BEACON SER SERIES

SERMON OUTLINES

— ON —

The Book of Luke

DERL G. KEEFER

Beacon Hill Press of Kansas City
Kansas City, Missouri

Copyright 2003
by Beacon Hill Press of Kansas City

ISBN 083-412-064X

Printed in the
United States of America

Cover Design: Paul Franitza

10   9   8   7   6   5   4   3   2   1

CONTENTS

The Christmas Story

Luke 1—2

Introduction

Everyone loves a good story! The ingredients of a great story include entertainment, revelation, feeling, and insight. The Christmas scripture includes all the drama and ingredients for a wonderful and insightful story that rivets our attention for eternity.

I. The Christmas Story Is Entertaining

A. The Christmas story contains the drama of a young teenager being engaged to an older man. He discovers that his fiancé has "miraculously" become pregnant and they attempt to deal with this situation.

B. The Christmas story contains a variety of characters as part of the drama.

  1. Wise men travel from a distant land in order to discover a new king born in Israel. Imagine all the emotions, dialogue, and experiences they encountered along their journey.

  2. The appearance of angels adds to the "spectacular" effects of the story.

  3. Shepherds in their fields add to the "human" element of this story.

II. The Christmas Story Has an Author

A. The story's byline reads *God!*

B. The introduction of a baby into the story of a lifetime comes from the very heart of God. He writes the human element into the story. The beginning is not a decree or a journey or the mother/father relationship; not the angels; but rather, the creator of the universe who has a compassionate heart for a rebellious people. He authors the story.

III. The Christmas Story Has a Plot

A. The plot of the story is nothing less than the redemption of the planet.

B. The plot of the story brings to life the ultimate redemption and completion of the cosmic salvation of the world and its inhabitants for eternity.

C. The plot of the story demonstrates that annihilation and destruction can be avoided because the author writes in the character of salvation.

D. The plot introduces a tiny baby who becomes a man and this man . . . becomes the sacrifice for the salvation of the world.

Sometime ago I took a tour of the United Nations building. In the regular meeting chamber of the Security Council of the United Nations was a large mural on the wall with the theme "War and Peace." At the bottom its colors are somber and the symbolism depicts discord, strife, and hatred. As one's eyes travel up the wall, one discovers the colors become brighter and the symbolism less hostile and more cooperative. The pinnacle of the picture is unfinished as the artist wanted to depict that the best is yet to come. The dark and bloody past is a prologue to the fairer and friendlier future. The theme depicts the Christmas story. The redemption of the world comes by way of a dark past of sin and rebellion to a friendlier and fairer future.

IV. The Christmas Story Has a Climax

A. The future climax of eternity must pass through the brutality of Calvary . . . the crucifixion of Jesus.

B. The future climax of eternity must pass through the agony of a painful death.

C. The future climax of eternity must pass through the glory of an empty tomb because of the resurrection of the body.

D. The future climax of eternity is just the beginning of forever!

Conclusion

The Christmas story is a love story; its author is love, its plot is love, its purpose is love. In Jesus' birth, life, teachings, death, and resurrection we have the full revelation of the love of God. Our Christmas carol is the adoration and submission to Christ.

The Ultimate Question

Luke 1:57-80

Introduction

The birth of John the Baptist prepared the way for the birth of Jesus. Later on his ministry prepared the way for Christ's own ministry. Jesus said of John that among those born of women, none was greater than John the Baptist. He was to prepare the Israelites for the ultimate question that Jesus came to ask . . . In whom is life to begin?

I. **The Ultimate Question Is Influenced by Others**
   A. The neighbors could be an influence (v. 66).
   B. The parents could be an influence.
   C. You are a child of God and you are worth life itself.

II. **The Ultimate Question Actively Involves the New Covenant**

   Zachariah launches into the Benedictus or blessing. It extends from verses 68-79.
   A. Praise to God for the messianic deliverance (vv. 68-75).
      1. Celebration for the significant role John will have in this work of the Kingdom
      2. Celebration for the significant influence John will have in this work of the Kingdom
      3. Celebration for the significant hope John will have in this work of the Kingdom
   B. Praise for the new covenant the Messiah offers (vv. 69-72)
      1. The Messiah will offer salvation.
      2. The Messiah will offer strength.
      3. The Messiah will offer power.

III. **The Ultimate Question Is a Personal Decision to Follow and Obey God**
   A. Obedience marked the character of Zachariah.
      1. His obedience caused healing to happen—his speech returned.

2. His obedience caused a celebration to erupt.
3. His obedience caused worship to occur.
B. Following God marked the character of Zachariah.
    1. He followed God in righteous living.
    2. He followed God with a conscious decision.
    3. He followed God and was filled with the Spirit.
    4. He followed God and was rewarded with a prophetic son.

Conclusion

The good news is that we can be born again with all the joy and promise that attended the birth of John the Baptist.

A New Voice for an Old Need—Righteousness

Luke 3:1-20

Introduction

Luke opens his narrative by reminding his audience of secular and religious voices of the past who would figure into the scheme of Christ's story. The Gospel writer focused on the star of the story, Jesus, and how He would influence the people. Luke wants his readers to be acquainted with people like Tiberius Caesar (Caesar being a title and not a person) who began his reign after the death of Augustus in A.D. 14.

Fifteen years later (Luke 3:1) puts the date of this event at approximately A.D. 20. This Herod is Herod Antipas, the son of Herod the Great, ruler of Galilee and Perea from 4 B.C. to A.D. 39. Herod Antipas's half brother, Philip, ruled a group of territories to the northeast of Palestine, Iturea, and Traconitis (4 B.C. to A.D. 33/34). Only a few inscriptions give a clue to another name in our text, Lysanias. Pontius Pilate was governor of Judea from A.D. 26 to 36 and Luke's readers would later become much better acquainted with Pilate.

In addition to the secular voices of the day, Luke presents the religious voices. He introduces the reader to Annas, whose official high priestly duties ended in A.D. 15. Annas, however, continues as an "unofficial" adviser to his son-in-law, Caiaphas, who served as high priest in Israel from A.D. 18 to 36.

Neither the secular nor religious voices of the day called for a moving away from the evil practices of the day. The unvarnished truth revealed that both the secular and religious voices epitomized evil in all of its unholy forms. A new voice arose from the rubble of the day. This voice called for truth, righteousness, and an amputation of evil from the lives of the people. It came through the voice of John the Baptist. Luke's hope was that in the text the voice of John would travel through human history and land at the heart's listening ear of people throughout all ages.

Listening to the Voice of a Prophet

    A. A prophet—a messenger for truth
       1. A messenger of truth to discern God's purpose
       2. A messenger of truth to discern God's action
       3. A messenger of truth to discern God's judgment
       4. A messenger of truth to discern God's grace
    B. A prophet—a messenger to the needy
       1. A messenger of awareness
       2. A messenger of repentance
       3. A messenger of remedy
    C. A prophet—a messenger to the receptive heart
       1. A receptive heart turns from evil
       2. A receptive heart turns from sinfulness
       3. A receptive heart turns from uselessness

Conclusion

I read about a young man who entered a bank many years ago in New York City to apply for a loan. After completing the forms he was surprised that it took so long for a reply. He was becoming anxious as he noticed that the loan officer kept going to the manager's desk.

Finally the paperwork was completed and as he rose to leave, suddenly flashbulbs began flashing in his face and people began crowding around him. He thought that he must have done something wrong and that look appeared on his face. However, he was relieved to learn that instead of doing something wrong, he had been "lucky" enough to be at the right place at the right time. The bank manager handed his loan papers back with the reply that he would not have to repay the loan. The money he had borrowed included the one-billionth dollar ever loaned by that bank. In honor of that fact, his debt would never be written in the books; he would never be required to repay it.

John told the people that a Redeemer was coming to do for them what occurred to the young man in the bank. Jesus Christ, who was coming to take their debts and remove the sin obligation from the books, was on the way! Sin, placed on Jesus, would never be held against anyone who would accept Jesus into his or her life because Jesus would pay the cost of the loan! What was true for them would be true for all people of all ages.

A NEW OVERCOMING POWER

Luke 3:21; 4:1-13

Introduction

The desert experience in Luke 4 would tempt Jesus to forsake the road of suffering. If Satan could get Jesus, early on, to deny His calling, the world would go on without a true Messiah. Christ's temptation marks His initiation into ministry. This incident reaffirms our faith that there is an overcoming power to resist temptation, Satan, and sin.

I. **Overcoming Power Is Connected to the Person of Jesus**
   A. The overcoming power of Jesus over Satan
      1. The seducing life of Satan
      2. The seducing subtlety of Satan
      3. The seducing strategy of Satan
      4. The seducing compromise of Satan
      5. The seducing promises of Satan
   B. The transforming power of Jesus over temptation
      1. Temptation of the mind
      2. Temptation of the sensual desires
      3. Temptation of the spirit
      4. Temptation of the body
         Horace Mann said, "Temptation is a fearful word. It indicates the beginning of a possible series of infinite evils. It is the ringing of an alarm bell, whose melancholy sounds may reverberate through eternity. Like the sudden, sharp cry of 'Fire!' under our windows by night, it should rouse us to instantaneous action, and brace every muscle to its highest tension."[1]
   C. The transforming power of Jesus over sin
      1. Sin is separation from God.
      2. Sin is the inclination to do wrong.
      3. Sin is the notion that "I am in charge."
         Hugh Calkins wrote, "Sin that damns is a mindset

which means awareness and conscious choice of self-worship instead of God-worship."[2]

II. Transforming Power Is Connected to Obedience

A. Obedience is offering self to God.
B. Obedience is offering sacrificially to God.
C. Obedience is offering immediately to God.
D. Obedience is offering success to God.

III. Transforming Power Is Connected to Worship

A. Worship is a need in the Christian's heart.
B. Worship is adoration in the Christian's heart.
C. Worship is praise in the Christian's heart.
D. Worship is glory in the Christian's heart.
E. Worship is full attention to God in the Christian's heart.

Conclusion

John Bakewell penned these words, circa 1757:

> Hail, Thou once despised Jesus!
> Hail, Thou Galilean King!
> Thou didst suffer to release us;
> Thou didst free salvation bring.
> Hail, Thou agonizing Saviour,
> Bearer of our sin and shame!
> By Thy merits we find favor;
> Life is given thro' Thy name.
> Paschal Lamb, by God appointed,
> All our sins on Thee were laid.
> By almighty love anointed,
> Thou hast full atonement made;
> All Thy people are forgiven
> Thro' the virtue of Thy blood.
> Opened is the gate of heaven;
> Peace is made 'twixt man and God.[3]

1. G. B. F. Hallock, *Five Thousand Best Modern Illustrations* (New York: Richard R. Smith, Inc., 1931), 682.

2. Albert Wells, Jr., *Inspiring Quotations* (Nashville: Thomas Nelson, 1988), 187.

3. John Bakewell, "Hail, Thou Once Despised Jesus!" in *Praise and Worship* (Kansas City: Nazarene Publishing House, 1951), 85.

The Gospel According to Jesus

Luke 4:16-20

Introduction
  This passage is a grand summation of the gospel according to Jesus!

I. **Jesus Came to Preach Good News!**
  A. Good news to the poor—those who lacked resources for a fruitful life.
  B. Good news to the guilt ridden—those who could be forgiven.
  C. Good news to the person who is afraid of death—those who could find life in the resurrection.

II. **Jesus Came to Preach the Good News of "Release to the Captive" Hearts**
  A. Release of the captive hearts of the past
    1. Release of the past prejudice
    2. Release of the past hatred
    3. Release of the past sin
  B. Release of the captive hearts of the present
    1. Those conformed to the patterns of sinful habits
    2. Those conformed to the patterns of sinful attitudes
    3. Those conformed to the patterns of sinful behavior
  C. Release of the captive hearts of the future
    1. Fear of the uncertainty of the unknown
    2. Fear of the uncertainty of death
  D. Release of the captives to bring hope
    1. Hope through a resurrection
    2. Hope through relevant faith
    3. Hope through an everlasting life

III. **Jesus Came to Preach Good News to the Sightless**
  A. The physical sightless
  B. The social sightless
  C. The resurrection sightless
  D. The spiritual sightless

IV. Jesus Came to Preach Good News to the Prisoners

A. Jesus came to set free those prisoners in bondage of time.

B. Jesus came to set free those prisoners in bondage to silence.

C. Jesus came to set free those prisoners in bondage of turmoil.

D. Jesus came to set free those prisoners in bondage to purposelessness.

Conclusion

Chuck Swindoll recounts in his devotional book *Day by Day* that our nation's first institution of higher learning was founded in 1636 and named for a minister of the gospel by the name of John Harvard. His untimely death in 1637 resulted in his library being donated to help the fledgling college in Cambridge. The purpose of Harvard was to train Christian ministers for generations to come.

According to Swindoll, these facts help explain the original Harvard seal: a shield including three opened books, two facing up, the third facing down, and the Latin words *Veritas Christo et Ecclesiae*—"Truth for Christ and the Church."

It was a constant reminder to students for all generations that truth and freedom only come in Jesus Christ. The seal displayed three books representing the importance of knowledge—yet with the one turned down it demonstrated the limitations of human understanding and reason.

Within the last several decades, that godly philosophy of education eroded and the new seal carries no reference to Christ or his church. The book that faced down now faces up and represents that intellect is everything and there are no divine mysteries.

Swindoll writes, "There is a nasty fly in this humanistic ointment, however. It's the D word: Depravity. The sinfulness of the human heart is not altered by the pursuit of knowledge."[1]

Jesus has come to bring the good news that the pursuit of His gospel will set us free!

---

1. Charles Swindoll, *Day by Day* (Nashville: Word Publishing, 2000), 244.

Jesus Brings a New View

Luke 4:14-44

Introduction

Jesus returns from the desert yielded to the Father, conqueror over the devil, and victorious over temptation. An intense sense of God's destiny filters into the heart and mind of Jesus as He feels "called" to tell the world the good news of salvation. He launches this worldwide view from Galilee. He delivers a new sermon, new theology, new view at the synagogue in His hometown. It spans time and reaches to people in this day.

I. Jesus' New Sermon Was Preached (vv. 14-22)

A. His sermon was preached in the power of the Spirit.
   1. The spirit of truth
   2. The spirit of action
   3. The spirit of activity
   4. The spirit of philosophy
   5. The spirit of words
B. His sermon fleshed out the prophet Isaiah's sermon of the plight of sinners.
   1. The sinner is spiritually poor. The sinner is spiritually bankrupt and has no source to bring about salvation. Only Jesus can do that.
   2. The sinner is spiritually jailed. Sinners then and sinners today have been taken prisoner by Satan. They cannot break free from Satan, from bad habits, from negative attitudes. Only Jesus can unlock spiritual prison doors!
   3. The sinner is spiritually blind. Satan gouges out people's spiritual sight. No longer can they see God's hand in the world or working in their life.

      Living near the Kentucky border, I heard about fish that exist in an exceptionally large cave that stretched for several miles in an underground river. The fish are blind. They have eyes but cannot see. They have lived in darkness so long that their eyes are of no value.

Sinners become so accustomed to spiritual darkness that their spiritual sight is gone. Only Jesus can restore their spiritual eyes to normalcy.

4. The sinner is spiritually oppressed. Satan will do anything to force people down or burden them with unbearable loads, but Jesus provides freedom!

II. Jesus' New Sermon Was Rejected (vv. 23-30)

A. Rejected for selfish reasons
B. Rejected for irrational reasons
C. Rejected for traditional reasons
D. Rejected for "religious" reasons

Someone noted that the Bible never says that Jesus ever returned to Nazareth. Rejection can be final! What a sorrowful commentary on the people.

III. Jesus' New Sermon Was Demonstrated (vv. 31-44)

A. Jesus demonstrated His love through authority.
1. People recognized His authority over demons.
2. People recognized His authority over spiritual powers.
3. People rejected His authority in action.
4. People rejected His authority in love.
B. Jesus demonstrated His love through compassion.
1. Jesus' compassion should be a consistent quality in Christians.
2. Jesus' compassion should be a consistent lifestyle for the Christian.
3. Jesus' compassion should be a consistent unlocking of social, economic, and racial prison doors.

Conclusion

There are many sermons to preach to our world—sermons on deliverance, social justice, healing, peace, and more. Whatever we preach must be lived before others so they can see the gospel demonstrated.

A New Catch!

Luke 5:1-11

Introduction

Discipleship exceeds the minimum requirement of believing with the head, for it demands involvement. Jesus conveys this to Simon Peter in the text when He tells Peter he would "catch men" in verse 10. People must not be "caught" without personal involvement in their lives. Jesus told Simon and his crew that just as their fishnets were barren, so were their lives; but, the good news was that their fishnets were to become full, so also would their lives! We often feel empty, alone, unwanted, and unsatisfied, but then Jesus steps into our boats and tells us to launch out deeper.

As we obey Him, our nets will be filled with satisfaction. We will call others to share in the excitement.

I. Discipleship Includes Listening

A. Listening is a conscious effort to hear what is being said.
1. It involves paying close attention to what is being said.
2. It involves being influenced by what is being said.
3. It involves being persuaded by what is being said.

B. Listening is demonstrating a desire to change what is happening in our lives.

C. Listening is being practical in our desire to hear God.
1. I listen by reading God's Word.
2. I listen by reading devotional materials written by godly people.
3. I listen by being counseled by mature individuals.
4. I listen by being morally, ethically, and spiritually insightful.

II. Discipleship Includes an Encounter with Jesus

It sounds simple to have an encounter with Jesus, but the hard, cold truth is that it isn't always easy. I need to speak to God. The exciting news is that God wants to speak to me! He waits patiently on me even when I'm running from one "to do list item" to the next. I must go where Jesus is waiting. Here are some practical ways to find Him.

    A. Pick a location.

    B. Pick a time.

    C. We must learn to fit into God's schedule and not demand our own schedule.

    D. Pick a reason.

III. Discipleship Includes Worship

    A. Worship is an outward act of humankind brought about by an inner awareness of our defect.

    B. Worship is a face-to-face encounter with God in corporate and individual settings.

    C. Worship is the awe of God in your heart and place of worship.

    D. Worship is the awareness of God's holiness.

    E. Worship is the accountability with fellow believers.

    F. Worship is praise and adoration to God.

IV. Discipleship Includes Abandonment of Self

    A. Abandonment of the fear of failure

    B. Abandonment of the fear of following

    C. Abandonment of the fear of focusing

    D. Abandonment of the fear of fellowship

V. Discipleship Includes Evangelism Sharing

    A. Sharing is refusing to hoard the love of God.

    B. Sharing is feeling the urgency to tell the good news about God.

    C. Sharing is giving hope for all eternity.

Conclusion

As Christians we face people daily who will step out into eternity with or without God. As disciples we must be prepared to share the wonderful news that Jesus can transform anyone's life who is willing to accept Him. The Great Commission compels us to participate in God's great master plan of evangelizing the world.

Levi—a New Risk

Luke 5:27-31

Introduction

Has anyone taken a risk on you lately? God has! Jesus came because God saw in us a tremendous potential for righteousness and holiness that the world overlooked. No one liked Levi. He was despised by his fellow citizens and exploited by his employers. He was never asked to sit in on table games in a respectful home. However, he was rich and powerful. He had some friends, but they were also looked down on by the common people in the town. He was put in the same class as murderers, pickpockets, thieves, and burglars. He could never be a witness at a trial, nor ever be a lawyer. Few liked him!

Most people in his profession were well-educated and knew several languages. There was a knack for understanding numbers, and his kind worked them well. He owned several pieces of property. It was *how* he earned his money that bothered most individuals. He was considered a traitor to his people and to his country. They looked on him as immoral. His name was Levi, and he was a tax collector for the occupying forces of Rome. He skimmed money off the top and bottom and enforced his dishonesty with Roman force. Yet, this was a man in whom Jesus saw the potential to become one of His disciples. He was a person who would help change the world for Jesus!

I. Levi Was a Man with a Future

A. Jesus offered to look beyond his past instead of condemning him.

B. Jesus offered grace instead of guilt. "Grace is Christianity's best gift to the world, a spiritual nova in our midst exerting a force stronger than vengeance, stronger than racism, stronger than hate" (Philip Yancey).[1]

C. Jesus offered leadership instead of a mindless following.

D. Jesus offered freedom to envision a released heart.

E. Jesus offered hope in a hopeless situation. "Hope. It is something as important to us as water is to a fish, as vital as electricity is to a light bulb, as essential as air is to a jumbo jet. Hope is basic to life.

"We cannot stay on the road to anticipated dreams without it, at least not very far. Many have tried—none successfully. Without that needed spark of hope, we are doomed to a dark, grim existence" (Charles Swindoll).[2]

II. Levi Was a Man of Gratitude

A. He was rejected by everyone but accepted by Christ.

B. He was renewed in life by the transforming power of Christ.

C. He was grateful for a new friend and a new Savior in Christ.

1. Gratitude for what Christ gave—salvation
2. Gratitude for what Christ gave—a commission to follow
3. Gratitude for what Christ gave—a call to everyone

III. Levi Was a Man with Another Name—Matthew

A. Matthew means "gift of God."

B. Matthew became a reflector of God.

"In the late 1700s, a man named Ami Argand invented a parabolic reflector, a device that intensified a lighthouse's beams. Thin sheets of copper were molded into shape of parabolas to form the reflectors, and these were then covered with silver to reflect the light more brilliantly. The reflectors were placed behind the lamp and could be adjusted to focus the light where needed. "Our hearts, too, can be like silver, curved around the light of Christ, ready to focus His love wherever it is needed."[3]

C. Matthew had a new destination in life and forever.

Conclusion

Jesus passes by all and asks us to respond to His call to follow. Are you ready to risk all and follow Him?

1. Philip Yancey, *What's So Amazing About Grace?* (Grand Rapids: Zondervan Publishing House, 1997), 30.

2. Charles Swindoll, *Hope Again* (Dallas: Word Publishing, 1996), 3.

3. Ellyn Sanna, *A Beacon of Hope* (Uhrichsville, Ohio: Barbour Publishing, Inc., 2000), 33.

A New Prime Interest Rate

Luke 6:1-3

Introduction

Once a month a major event occurs around my house that drives my accountant wife crazy—it is balancing my checkbook! While at the computer working on my accounting program I usually yell out, "Honey, my checkbook doesn't balance—again!" When we were first married she gasped in horror at what I was doing. I really couldn't understand her feelings because I had always done it that way before—writing the balance on the bank statement in my checkbook when it came. It certainly saved a lot of time!

Slowly (after 34 years of marriage) I'm learning the terms. It may not actually help me balance my checkbook, but at least I know the terms.

One principle I believe is that money should be a source of happiness. It should be used to bring happiness to the family, neighbors, and the world around me. How I use my money reveals the type of person I am, generous or stingy.

What I own has been entrusted to me from Almighty God, and He expects me to use it wisely. His plan for my life includes my billfold, checkbook, time, and talent.

The text is in parabolic form and hacks its way into our motive for using God's money. Jesus emphasized the point when He states, "No slave can serve two masters; for a slave will either *hate* the one and *love* the other, or be devoted to the one and despise the other." Then he hammers home the point, "You cannot serve both God and Money" (Luke 16:13).

Christ's parable reveals the opportunity for the right use of material items. What is our prime interest? Has Jesus given you a new prime interest?

I. Our New Prime Interest Is the Wise Use of Time

   A. Time allows me to keep in step with God.

   B. Time allows me to step back and catch the right perspective.

   C. Time allows me to learn the right priorities.

D. Time allows me to heal hurts and begin forgiveness.

E. Time allows me to use it as a tool to work for the Kingdom.

F. Time allows me to understand it is mine and God's.

John Maxwell has two foundation biblical principles for time management that he shares: (1) Realize that you have enough time to do all that God wants you to do. (2) Come apart and rest or you'll come apart. Dr. Maxwell then counsels, "The best remedy for a schedule that is out of control is to get alone with God and practice principle #1."[1]

II. Our New Prime Interest Is the Priority of Life

A. The prime interest of life is to develop into people who please God.

B. The prime interest of life is to prioritize our thinking process to please God.

C. The prime interest of life is to prioritize our attitudes toward life for God.

D. The prime interest of life is to prioritize our actions in life for God.

We need to prioritize our actions. What we *do* substantiates the thought process and attitudes. God calls each person to be holy in an unholy world. Somewhere I read that Dag Hammarskjöld, the late United Nations president, said, "The road to holiness necessarily passes through the world of action."

III. Our New Prime Interest Is the Wise Use of Money

A. Money should bring contentment, not covetousness.

B. Money should assist our lifestyle of service to others.

C. Money should aid in honoring God.

"There are many things that money cannot buy. Money can buy: A bed but no sleep. Books but not brains. Food but not an appetite. Finery but not beauty. A house but not a home. Medicine but not health. Pleasures but not peace. Luxuries but not culture. Amusements but not joy. A crucifix but not a Savior. A church building but not heaven."[2]

---

1. John Maxwell, *One Hour with God* (San Diego: Injoy, Inc., 1994), n.p.

2. Charles Swindoll, *The Tale of the Tardy Oxcart* (Nashville: Word Publishing, 1998), 391.

A New Start Through Healing

Luke 7:1-17

Introduction

Dr. James Dobson wrote a book in 1993 titled *When God Doesn't Make Sense.* He writes about the difficulties, inexplicable sorrows, and illness that happen to God's people. He observes, "Wars, famines, diseases, natural disasters, and untimely deaths are never easy to rationalize. But large-scale miseries of this nature are sometimes less troubling to the individual than the circumstances that confront each of us personally, such as cancer, kidney failure, heart disease, sudden infant death syndrome, cerebral palsy, Down's syndrome, divorce, rape, loneliness, rejection, failure, infertility, widowhood! These and a million other sources of human suffering produce inevitable questions that trouble the soul. 'Why would God permit this to happen to me?' It is a question all believers—and many pagans—have struggled to answer. And contrary to Christian teachings in some circles, the Lord typically does not rush in to explain what He is doing."[1]

So what are we to do? How do we find healing of body, mind, emotions, and spirit in circumstances like these? The scripture lesson gives clues to the principles in our need of healing.

I. A Key Principle of Healing Is Faith

A. Faith includes courage to believe even when we are in a fog as to the outcome.

B. Faith includes strength to believe even when we are in a fog as to the outcome.

C. Faith includes humility to believe even when we are in a fog as to the outcome.

D. Faith includes expectance to believe even when we are in a fog as to the outcome.

E. Faith includes trust to believe even when we are in a fog as to the outcome.

Charles Spurgeon said, "If we cannot believe God when circumstances seem to be against us, we do not believe Him at all."[2]

23

The miracle of life and living would be absolutely transformed if we could only have a faith like the centurion's. Fear and mistrust have imprisoned us far too long. Faith in Jesus must be an implicit trust in His great power and ability, not only for deliverance from physical ailments but also for the daily transformation of our living. Have you saluted Jesus by making Him the object of your faith?

II. A Key Principle of Healing Is Compassion

A. Acknowledge God's presence in compassion for others.
B. Affirm openness in compassion in dealing with others.
   1. Open to others in spite of your own preset ideas
   2. Open to others in spite of what people might think
   3. Open to others in spite of hurts
C. Assist others in becoming people of compassion to bring healing into focus.
D. Assume a posture of hope in our compassion to others.
   The old hymn the "Balm of Gilead" reminds us of an ointment that healed the wounds of the people. Jesus, known for His compassion, became identified as the "balm of Gilead." Christ's followers should also be recognized as carriers of the "balm" of compassion.

III. A Key Principle of Healing Is Understanding

A. Understanding through our actions in helping others
B. Understanding through exposing our feelings in helping others
C. Understanding through revealing our need to others
D. Understanding through loving those in need

Conclusion

The ingredients are blended together—faith, compassion, and understanding—ready to bring healing to others. Your commission today is to take all those ingredients as a balm to those in need of healing!

1. James Dobson, *When God Doesn't Make Sense* (Wheaton, Ill.: Tyndale House Publishers, Inc., 1993), 7-8.

2. Albert Wells, Jr. *Inspiring Quotations* (Nashville: Thomas Nelson Publishers, 1988), 68.

A Liberating Day

Luke 7:36-50

Introduction

The sun shone brightly and there wasn't a cloud in the sky. The day was to be perfect and festive rolled into one. All day long people in multicolored robes paraded in and out of Simon's house preparing for a great feast. The servants placed the couches in proper order and the tables were lined with great Eastern Oriental food. A party mood pervaded the house. The time for the banquet arrived, and everyone who was anyone was present, including Jesus and His disciples. It was Jesus that Simon had intentionally invited so that he could become better acquainted with this itinerant young rabbi. Simon had heard from many that this man was a prophet, but he wanted to test the truth of it for himself.

Everything seemed to be going smoothly as they ate and laughed—milling around the room, reclining at the tables, and having a good party time! Since everyone in the community was invited to the party, no one noticed her. If anyone was looking at her, they noticed a searching look in her eyes, but it ended when she saw Jesus. Around her neck she wore the traditional alabaster flask of perfumed oil. It had no handles and was furnished with a long neck, which was broken off when the contents were needed. Possibly she had listened to Jesus speak on several occasions and felt a deep need in her heart. She had a notorious reputation that followed her everywhere, but when He preached she felt that her life could be changed. Who knows when it happened, but on one of those preaching tours Jesus had given her life a chance to change. Her gratitude had mounted to fever pitch. When she heard that Jesus would be at Simon's, she planned to be there to tell Him of her eternal gratitude. As she approached Jesus she was overcome with emotion that would not let her speak. Gripped by her emotions, the tears ran freely from her eyes and onto the feet of Jesus. When she realized that she had no towel to wipe His feet, she did something that no Jewish woman would do—she loosed her hair and wiped His feet. She was oblivious to all others and focused intently on Jesus. In the emotions of the moment she began kissing His feet in gratitude that He had set her free. Then in a flash she broke open her perfumed ointment from the flask and began applying it to His feet as a symbolic act of servitude. She made a public spectacle of herself!

Simon was appalled at the sight, but we are not told of his outward action. We are told by Luke of his mental reaction. He judged the nonaction of Jesus. (Read Luke 7:39.) Bruce Larson writes, "We don't know how Simon reacted, but he is exposed. He knew everything about religion, liturgy, theology, ethics, temple worship, and the law. He knew all about the things of God but somehow he missed the essence of it all, which this woman captured."[1]

I. A Defining Moment of Liberation Comes When We Acknowledge Our Sinfulness
  A. Sin is a waste of life.
  B. Sin is a parched and barren life.
  C. Sin is a purposeless life.
  D. Sin is a Christless life.
  E. Sin is a fraud to life.

II. A Defining Moment of Life Comes When We Are Convicted of Our Sinfulness
  A. Conviction is realizing we have hurt God himself.
  B. Conviction is realizing whom we have rebelled against.
  C. Conviction is realizing where our loyalty should be established.
  D. Conviction is realizing for whom we would die.

III. A Defining Moment a Matter of Faith
  A. A saving moment of faith decision
  B. A saving moment to walk by faith and not by sight
  C. A saving moment to minister by faith
  D. A saving moment to relationally cooperate with God

---

1. Bruce Larson, *Communicator's Commentary* (Waco: Word Book Publishers, 1983), 139.

A Life-Changing Encounter

Luke 8:26-39

Introduction

From Capernaum in Galilee Jesus and His disciples sailed to the southeast shore of the lake to the area of the Gadarenes. A demon-possessed man wandered constantly among the tombs of the town. Few people walked that way because he would come out naked and confused and attack any passersby. Jesus and His men docked their boat near the tombs. The man ran out to molest them but instead walked away from the encounter a changed man, because he met Jesus!

I. He Had a Changing Encounter

A. He was devil-possessed.
  1. The job of the devil is to destroy.
  2. The job of the devil is to entice.
B. He became Jesus-possessed.
  1. The job of Jesus is to give life.
  2. The job of Jesus is to give eternal life.

II. He Had an Uplifting Encounter

A. He had been in an oppressive state of life.
  1. Habits that defiled him
  2. Attitudes that defeated him
  3. Complacency that destroyed him
B. He had been in a terrifying state of life.
C. He encounters Jesus, who returns him to his right state of heart and of mind.

III. He Had a Converting Encounter

A. Saw himself for what he really was in life
B. Enlightened by God's divine light
C. Discovered that he could only be delivered by God's power
D. Identified with the only Source of help available to break his bondage

IV. He Had a Settling Encounter
A. Sin causes confusion.
1. Sin has life's emphasis on the wrong things.
2. Sin has life's priorities in the wrong place.
3. Sin has life lost.
B. Salvation causes a settling in life.
1. Salvation settles the issues of life.
2. Salvation settles the prioritizing of life.
3. Salvation settles the moral issues of life.

V. He Had a Loving Encounter
A. Jesus lovingly encounters his loneliness by offering himself to be his friend.
B. Jesus lovingly encounters his tough question of, "What have I to do with You, Jesus, Son of the Most High God?" (v. 28, NKJV).
C. Jesus lovingly encounters his need and sends the demon away.

VI. He Had a Satisfying Encounter
A. His satisfaction is in the authority that Jesus brings, and the man now decides to act responsibly.
B. His satisfaction is in the wholeness that Jesus brings, and the man now decides to act with morals.
C. His satisfaction is in the healing that Jesus brings, so he is no longer paranoid and decides to act in life with feeling.

Conclusion
There are other characters in this story—the townspeople. After seeing the devil-released man sitting in his right mind at the feet of Jesus, the Bible says that they were afraid and asked Jesus to leave their territory. What a tragedy! The townspeople represent the sinful world of unbelievers. They fear the truth about God, others, and possibly even themselves. I wonder how many of us today are like the devil-released man who accepts Christ's healing. How many of us are like the townspeople who ask Jesus to leave us alone. Please, friends, don't turn Jesus away!

MULTIPLICATION MINISTRY

Luke 9:1-6

Introduction

Many churches qualify for an "ingrown church" look. What is needed is an outward look toward ministry. There are a variety of programs within the church with the overarching sign, MINISTRY. Each one works in cooperation within the Church of Jesus Christ for His glory and His honor coupled with a deeply compassionate heart that reaches out to others. The ministry areas include:

I. The Ministry of Evangelism

A. The proclamation of the saving work of Jesus Christ

B. The proclamation of the sanctifying work of the Holy Spirit

C. The proclamation of the satisfying work of a lifetime of experience

D. The proclamation of the work contains perils

   1. Complacency

      "I have played enough sports, been in touch with enough coaches, watched enough games, and read closely enough to know that there's one strategy that's deadly. And it's so subtle. You think you can win by doing it, but you lose. It's called sitting on the lead. If you're an athlete or a sportsman, you know what I'm talking about. When I was in high school, our basketball team went to state finals in Texas. In one state final game we were ahead at halftime 26 to 18. The coach said, 'Now we got 'em. We got 'em. Just take it easy.' You know what? We lost, 41 to 40. Why? Because we tried to sit on our lead. We thought we had them beat, so we played with a maintenance mentality. A growing church never gets so far ahead that it can afford to 'sit on the lead.' Complacency is a major peril to evangelism."[1]

2. Loss of responsibility

"The evangelistic harvest is always urgent. The destiny of men and of nations is always being decided. Every generation is strategic. We are not responsible for the past generation, and we cannot bear the full responsibility for the next one; but we do have our generation. God will hold us responsible as to how well we fulfill our responsibilities to this age and take advantage of our opportunities."[2]

II. The Ministry of Teaching

The disciples were given authority to preach. Part of that preaching process incorporates teaching.

A. Teaching is developing disciples intellectually.
B. Teaching is developing disciples spiritually.
C. Teaching is developing disciples communally.

Ruffini wrote, "The teacher is like the candle which lights others in consuming itself."[3]

III. The Ministry of Availability

A. The ministry of availability of time
B. The ministry of availability of money
C. The ministry of availability of talent
D. The ministry of availability of spiritual gifts

Conclusion

God has given us talents and gifts to work together for Him. What a privilege we have to offer these talents and gifts to Christ, the church, the world, the lost, the needy. What an obligation God has bestowed on His people! We must never become spiritual misers and hoard what God has given us. Rather we must freely give it all away. When the prophet Samuel was a boy in the Temple he said, "Speak, Lord, your servant is listening." What is God speaking to you about regarding your talents and gifts? Are you listening and responding?

---

1. Charles Swindoll, *The Tale of the Tardy Oxcart* (Nashville: Word Publishing, 1998), 184.
2. Ibid., 183.
3. Hallock, *Five Thousand Best Modern Illustrations*, 680.

Moving Forward

Luke 9:57-62

Introduction

I heard about a minister who was walking by the seaside with his grandson. They stopped to watch the seagulls soar. An older man paused to watch the gulls as well. The two men began conversing and discovered that they both were clergymen who had served in the same area of the country earlier in their lives. The elderly gentleman shared his discontent with the church and life in general. He also had a slight touch of sunstroke. After a while the trio parted company. The grandson had been listening to all the complaints and a bit of the slurred speech of the elderly minister. As the two walked along the sandy seashore, the grandfather tried to explain that the older man had a sunstroke and was not feeling well. His grandson was quiet for a while thinking through what his grandfather said. He didn't quite grasp it all and it perplexed him. Finally he looked up to his grandfather and said, "Granddad, I hope you never suffer from sunset!" The Christian marches on, not to the sunset, but to the dawn. The watchword of the Kingdom is not "Backward" but "Forward!"

To the three men in the text, Jesus was saying, "I don't want lukewarm service because that is walking backward. I want a wholehearted commitment that moves you forward."

I. Moving Forward Is Counting the Cost of Discipleship

A. Counting the cost is seeing the broad picture of discipleship.

1. The broad picture doesn't allow for false pretense.
2. The broad picture demands a high standard beyond the commonplace.

   William Barclay wrote: "It may well be that we have hurt the Church seriously by trying to tell people that church membership need not make so very much difference; we would be better to tell them that it must make all the difference in the world. We might

31

have fewer people; but those we had would be totally pledged to Christ."[1]

   B. Counting the cost is seeing rejection as part of discipleship.

     1. It is not a life of glamour.

     2. It is not a life of zeal.

     3. It is not a life of ease.

     4. It is not a life of excitement.

     5. It is not a life of popularity.

       Discipleship can be brutal and full of rejection to those who misunderstand or refuse to believe the message of love and peace.

II. Moving Forward Is Seizing the Moment

Most commentators believe that the second man's father was not dead, but very much alive. The individual was saying, "I'll wait for a more convenient time maybe when my father is gone."

   A. Seizing the moment means that there comes a crucial moment of thought.

   B. Seizing the moment means that there comes a crucial moment of decision.

   C. Seizing the moment means that there comes a crucial moment of realizing that even the best excuse is no excuse.

   D. Seizing the moment means that there comes a crucial moment of action.

III. Moving Forward Is Catching the Vision

   A. The vision that looks beyond the horizons of life

   B. The vision that looks forward and not backward

   C. The vision that looks forward with a decisive step

   D. The vision that looks forward with a committed step

Conclusion

Tim Bowden, in his book *One Crowded Hour,* wrote about cameraman Neil Davis during the conflict between Malaysia and Indonesia in 1964. A group of Gurkhas from Nepal was asked to make an important decision. This special force group was asked if they would be willing to jump from transport planes into combat against the opposing Indonesian forces. The Gurkhas had the right to turn down the request because they had not been trained as paratroopers.

The Gurkhas normally agreed to each request the British made, but this time it was provisionally rejected. The following day one of the NCOs sought out the British officer who originally made the request and asked if the two of them could discuss the matter a bit more. The group had said that they would jump under certain conditions. The officer asked what those provisions were so he would see if he could accept them.

He was told that they would jump if the land were marshy or reasonably soft with no rocky terrain. They were inexperienced at jumping from planes.

The officer agreed. He asked if there was anything else. "Yes," the Gurkhas representative said. He requested that the plane fly as slowly as possible and no more than 100 feet high. The British officer pointed out the planes always flew as slowly as possible when dropping troops, but to jump from 100 feet was an impossibility. He informed the Gurkhas that the parachutes would not open in time from that height.

"Oh," said the Gurkhas, "that's all right, then. We'll jump with parachutes anywhere. You didn't mention parachutes before!"[2]

What Jesus wants are disciples with Gurkha-like commitment and courage to move their lives and the Kingdom forward!

---

1. William Barclay, *The Daily Study Bible—Luke* (Philadelphia: Westminster Press, 1953), 133.

2. Craig Larson, *Illustrations for Preaching and Teaching* (Grand Rapids: Baker Books, 1993), 36.

Neighbors for Eternity

Luke 10:25-37

Introduction

The text reveals the heart of a man who really did not want to be neighborly except to those *he* chose to be nice and neighborly to in life. This "expert in the law" defined a neighbor to be only a fellow Jew and no one else. He knew it was illegal to help a Gentile woman at the time of childbirth, for that was bringing another heathen Gentile into the world. Jesus saw through this man's insensitivity of humanity, and it irritated Him! Christ takes the opportunity to share one of His favorite teaching tools—the parable.

The parable is about a Jewish man who was beaten and left on the side of the road to die. Two religious leaders appear on the scene, a priest and a Levite. Both would be expected by Jesus' audience to stop and help the half-dead man. Jesus, however, throws a curve and depicts a Samaritan, a despised character by the Jewish people, as the compassionate one. It is the Samaritan who puts ointment on the wounds, bandages the man, puts him on his donkey, and takes him to the inn to find rest and healing. He even foots the bill for the stranger.

Jesus looks squarely into the eyes of the expert in the law and asks, "Who is the real neighbor?" The expert "sidestepper" refuses to mention the nationality of the compassionate man and says instead, "The one who showed mercy on him." Christ's piercing eyes stare straight into this lawyer's heart as He says to him, "Go and do likewise."

I. Jesus' Question of Neighborliness Involves Eternity

    A. Eternal life Christians are criticized as being so heavenly minded that they are of no earthly value.

    B. Eternal life involved treatment of people more than we realize.

    C. Eternal life is more than quantity of time.

    D. Eternal life is attitude of the heart.

        Etched over the three doorways of the Cathedral of

Milan are three inscriptions. Over one is carved a wreath of roses and written under them are the words, "All that pleases is but for a moment."

Over on the other side is sculpted a cross, with the words, "All that troubles is but a moment."

The central entrance in the main aisle has this truth inscribed, "That only is important which is eternal."[1]

II. Jesus' Question of Neighborliness Involves Intimacy
A. Intimacy involves relationship with others.
B. Intimacy involves helping others.
C. Intimacy involves caring about others.
D. Intimacy involves a positive attitude toward others.
> Our personal intimacy with God will help us in our intimacy with our neighbors.

III. Jesus' Question of Neighborliness Involves a Missionary Outlook
Maybe if we looked at the world as our neighbors we could live at peace rather than being belligerent and hateful toward other people. Some rules for right relationships with our neighbors in the world include:
A. Communicate positive feelings.
B. Communicate in-depth feelings.
C. Communicate by verbalizing feelings.
D. Communicate by attacking problems, not people.
E. Communicate directly, not indirectly.
F. Communicate with a forgiving spirit and not a judgmental spirit.

IV. Jesus' Question of Neighborliness Involves Action
A. How does action involve your lifestyle?
B. How does action involve people?
C. How does action involve your needs?

Conclusion
Who is *your* neighbor? Let us determine to build bridges of relationships, not obstacles to relationships!

---

1. Hallock, *Five Thousand Best Modern Illustrations,* 253.

Lessons from Two Sisters

Luke 10:38-42

Introduction

Jesus was on the road again to continue His preaching assignment when He stopped off in the tiny village of Bethany about three miles from Jerusalem. A woman named Martha welcomed Him and His disciples to her home with the enticement of a home-cooked meal. Jesus accepted!

Martha had a younger sister named Mary who she expected to help with the food preparation and serving. Sister Martha was slaving in the kitchen and Mary was helping. After a while Martha noticed that Mary was not helping anymore and wondered what had happened to her sister. Coming from the kitchen to the living room, she saw Mary sitting at Jesus' feet listening to the conversation swirling around her. Martha's disgust boiled inside her spirit. Ignoring Mary, Martha asked Jesus, "Lord, I'm doing all the work of cooking and serving and it's not getting done like I want it! Tell Mary to get herself up and get into the kitchen and help."

Jesus comes to the heart of the matter as He responds, "Martha, don't worry about it. I appreciate the food and hard work, but you and Mary are more important than the food. Don't be upset with Mary, but join us in conversation."

I'm so much like Martha! I see the work that needs to be done and feel I must rush in and do it. After all, if I don't do it—who will?

Which of the sisters is more like you? Martha, who needed to be working, or Mary, who felt like she should be listening? There are some lessons to be learned from this incident in the Scripture text.

Lesson 1: Misunderstanding Can Hurt

Martha misunderstood Christ's needs. She felt like she needed to be busy and work hard to make Him happy. All Jesus wanted was to have fellowship with her. He desired to teach her the important issues of life, but she was too busy. The bottom line issue for Martha was *priority.*

Chuck Swindoll in his book *Strengthening Your Grip* in 1982 wrote: "Here, in one sentence, is the warning: Don't let the urgent take the place of the important in your life. Oh, the urgent will really fight, claw, and scream for attention. It will plead for our time and even make us think we've done the right thing by calming its nerves. But the tragedy of it all is this: While you and I were putting out the fires of the urgent (an everyday affair), the important was again left in a holding pattern. And interestingly, the important is neither noisy nor demanding. Unlike the urgent, it patiently and quietly waits for us to realize its significance."[1]

Because Martha misunderstood the needs of Jesus, she was hurt. She should have asked Him what was important. When we have our perspective in line with Christ's, we can really serve in the proper sense.

- Be open to what others are saying, thinking, and needing.
- Be kind and tolerant in spirit and word. Compassion is a must!
- Be relevant to people in need.
- Be genuine. If we want to reach the generations in the 2000s, we must be transparent.
- Be integrity-oriented. Be reliable with what God has given you in life.
- Be spiritual. The foundation on all priority-based relationships for the Christian is that Christ is at the center of the heart and life and directs our spiritual journey.

Lesson 2: Desire to Understand Others As Well as Self

Martha needed to learn Mary's mysticism. Mary needed to learn Martha's pietism.

Martha's characteristics included independence, self-reliance, self-sufficiency, courage, logic, and "works" oriented.

Mary's characteristics included philosophical, visionary, idealism, thinker, sensitivity, enthusiastic, and emotional "faith" oriented.

A mystic in Christianity is one who chooses the inner world as a chamber of retreat with which to beautify the world. They retreat into themselves and opt for mystical meditation. Thought and quiet prayer is their forte.

A pietistic person is one who barges into the world. The inner chamber becomes the inner strength to charge into the world and take it for Jesus. "Being about the Father's business" is their motto for life. They would rather burn out than rust out.

What Martha and Mary needed was a blending of their traits. Working together to further the Kingdom through prayer and care becomes the lifestyle.

Lesson 3: Love, Love, Love!

There are different Greek words for love. One of them means a love for friends. Another is a love for family. A third word indicates a romantic love. There is one word that tells of God's great love for us. When He comes to reside in a person's heart, that godly love permeates the individual.

Do you have the kind of love that listens to the heart of God and reaches the heart of others?

---

1. Charles Swindoll, *Strengthening Your Grip* (Waco: Word Books, 1982), 17.

THE LIVING PRAYER

Luke 11:1-4

Introduction

Jesus had so much responsibility upon His broad shoulders. The weight of the world literally burdened Him to the point of fatigue and exhaustion with His daily schedule of travel, teaching, preaching, and small cell meetings with the Twelve or the Seventy. There was also the constant pressure of seeing human needs and the sincere desire to help relieve the distress of the people. Emotional pressure mounted with His almost daily conflicts with the Pharisees or the Sadducees.

A time of retreat became a necessary tool to keeping His sanity and focus. It is on such an occasion that we get a view of Jesus. Nothing specific is told, but the message comes over loud and clear.

The scripture relates that Jesus has pulled away from the crowds and that only the disciples are privy to Him. He has moved away from them to a lonely spot to pray. It is in this setting that we catch the deep expression of His spirit and communication with the Father. During His prayer time the disciples hear His cries and possibly catch some of the words. The disturbing problem was that they caught His spirit—something that they lacked. They longed for a prayer life that produced a live act, not some routine, static, or stagnant communication with God. These men knew that rabbis taught their students how to have a prayer life, and they craved that style of relationship with God. Jesus introduces them to the "living prayer."

"This is Luke's version of the Lord's Prayer. It is shorter than Matthew's, but it will teach us all we need to know about how to pray and what to pray for" writes William Barclay in his commentary on *The Gospel of Luke* (p. 145).

I. Our Living Prayer Brings Us to a Personal God

A. You have the privilege to call Him the parent—Father.
  1. God as an individual's parent
  2. God as a listening parent

3. God as a caring parent
4. God as a loving parent
5. God as a positive parent
6. God as an affectionate parent
7. God as a transparent parent

B. You have the privilege to call Him as the character—Father.
1. The character of God's mind
2. The character of God's heart
3. The character of God's integrity
4. The character of God's righteousness
5. The character of God's holiness
6. The character of God's justice
7. The character of God's love

II. Our Living Prayer Brings Us to Our Daily Need

A. Bread is the symbol of need
B. The present need
C. The sustainer of life in our need
D. The dependence of life in our need
E. The outlook of life in our need
F. The spiritual substance of life in our need
G. The bread to pass to our family in need

Notice that it is not "my daily bread, but rather, our daily bread." We receive the bread to share. We need to pass the bread at God's family table.

III. Our Living Prayer Brings Us to Forgiveness

A. We are under the penalty of the law of sin.
B. We have a defense attorney in Jesus.
C. We have the Cross, which brings us to the point of salvation.
D. We have the blood of Christ, which forgives and was shed for our forgiveness.
E. We have a Father who planned it that way.
F. We have the ability to reach out and receive His forgiveness.

Oswald Chambers writes, "The great miracle of the grace of God is that He forgives sin, and it is the death of Jesus Christ alone that enables the Divine nature to forgive and to remain true to itself in doing so. It is shallow nonsense to say that God forgives us because He is love. When we have been convicted of sin we will never say this again. The love of God means Calvary, and nothing less; the love of God is spelt on the Cross and nowhere else. The only ground on which God can forgive me is through the Cross of my Lord. There, His conscience is satisfied." Then he makes an important point on the idea of forgiveness when he states, "Forgiveness means not merely that I am saved from hell and made right for heaven . . . forgiveness means that I am forgiven into a recreated relationship, into identification with God in Christ. The miracle of Redemption is that God turns me, the unholy one, into the standard of Himself, the Holy One, by putting into me a new disposition, the disposition of Jesus Christ."[1]

IV. Living Prayer Brings Strength
    A. Strength to overcome temptation
    B. Strength to overcome sin
    C. Strength to know the difference between the two
    D. Strength to live and follow God

---

1. Oswald Chambers, *My Utmost for His Highest* (Uhrichsville, Ohio: Barbour and Company, Inc., 1963), 240-41.

The Prayers of Victory

Luke 18:1-14

Introduction

In this section of scripture Jesus uses parables as a source of instruction for His friends as well as for His enemies. I have laced the two together by their common threads and titled this sermon "The Prayers of Victory."

I. The Prayer of Victory Comes Through Persistence and Faith (vv. 4, 14)

A. Prayer goes nowhere if prayed without faith.

B. Prayer goes to God.

The woman in the story spoke to the judge many times. He was a ruthless man and an unjust judge. He was probably a paid magistrate appointed by either Herod or the Romans. If the plaintiff had no way to pay a bribe, he had no hope of getting his case settled. In his commentary William Barclay says that these officials were called "Judges of Prohibition or Punishment" (Dayyaneth Gezeroth), but that the people popularly called them "Robber Judges" (Dayyaneth Gezeloth). He could have denied her a hearing, but he states that because of her persistence she was wearing him out. It was that very persistence that won the victory.

Notice that Jesus is making a contrast here. If the judge does that for the woman, God will do that and more for His children.

1. The judge had no love for this woman and her cause, but God does.
2. The judge had no sense of propriety, but God does.
3. The judge had no compassion, but God does.
4. The judge had no authentic justice, but God does.

The publican's prayer calls for mercy from God. His faith was steadfast, unmoving, and unwavering, expressing praise to God. His concept of God was one of persistence, tenacity, resolution, and stubbornness that would not let go of humankind despite their wavering inconsistency. To the publican, prayer was a deep expression of the spirit—an experience of real communication with the Creator. Is it any wonder it was a prayer of victory?

II. The Prayer of Victory Comes with a Right Attitude (vv. 3, 14)

A. The woman and the publican came humbly to God—that's the right attitude.

B. The woman and the publican came expecting from God—that's the right attitude.

C. The woman and the publican came knowing God was in control—that's the right attitude.

D. The woman and the publican came to tap into the mind of God—that's the right attitude.

I believe it was Charles Swindoll who once said that words could never adequately convey the impact that attitude makes on life. The longer he lived the more convinced he became that life was 10% what happens to us and 90% how we respond to it.

III. The Prayer of Victory Comes by God's Mercy—Forgiving and Justifying (vv. 3, 14)

A. Victory in mercy
   1. Kindness
   2. Graciousness
   3. Looking beyond the wrong

B. Victory in forgiveness
   1. Letting go of our sin
   2. Letting our sin be covered by Christ's blood
   3. Letting our sin be sent as far as the east is from the west
   4. Letting our sin be removed as we are declared "righteous"

Conclusion

Paul in his Book to the Romans (4:7-8) quotes the psalmist by saying, "Blessed are they whose transgressions are forgiven, whose sins are covered. Blessed is the man whose sin the Lord will never count against him" (Ps. 32:1-2).

Freedom from a Sticky Life

Luke 19:1-10

Introduction

Mrs. Billie Cannon of Knoxville, Tennessee, needed her porch painted. She prepared her back porch by first applying a strip of adhesive double-edged tape around the edges. Her plan was to then place a drop cloth over the floor to protect it by securing it to the tape. After carefully placing the tape in its proper place, she went inside her home to retrieve the drop cloth. A few minutes later she was back outside ready to secure it, but found that all the tape was gone! She was mystified wondering who would possibly have taken the time to pull up all the tape. Her question also included the "why" of taking it up. She stood on the back porch puzzled by the predicament and mulling over the situation. In a few minutes she saw something in the backyard moving. Mrs. Cannon went over to investigate and discovered that it was a rather large snake rolling around. It was hopelessly enmeshed and immobilized in a large ball of tape! Evidently the snake had crawled up on the back porch and onto the tape while she was inside the house. The snake must have sensed the tape sticking to its skin and then began struggling only to get completely entangled in its own cellophane prison.

Someone commented that there are a lot of people like the snake. They have made a serious mistake, but rather than calmly analyzing their situation and correcting their course of action, they have reacted impulsively. Soon their lives are like that of the snake's—imprisoned in their own sticky tape of life.[1]

Our text deals with a man who had become imprisoned in the sticky state of life. He was immobilized psychologically, emotionally, financially, and spiritually. His name was Zacchaeus.

I. Freedom from the Sticky Situations of Life by Seeking Jesus

A. Freedom by overcoming obstacles

1. Overcoming obstacles by choosing loyalty to someone and not just a cause

  a. Choosing wisdom to serve the right person

  b. Choosing through common sense the right person

  c. Choosing the right priority for the right person

 2. Overcoming obstacles by picking the right challenges of life

  a. Pick the right causes.

  b. Pick the right time.

  c. Pick the right places.

  d. Pick the right reason.

B. Freedom by changing—changing our perspective

  Neil Anderson in an Internet devotional dated December 13, 2002, dealt with the alarming rate of changes that occurred during the end of the 20th century and the beginning of the 21st century. He noted that people are under a tremendous stress just to keep up with the rapid rate of change. He said that ministry challenge is to give these anxiety-ridden people the changeless message of Christ in a new and contemporary way that relates to a changing culture.

  He quotes Jesus in Luke 5:37 talking about not being able to put new wine into old wineskins. Anderson writes, "The wineskins don't represent the substance of faith; they represent the package our faith comes in. Christian practices wear out their purposes and the next generation doesn't relate to them." The truth is God is leading us into the 21st century, and our challenge is to learn how to adapt our worship, ministry, and style to a changing culture needing Jesus.

 1. Changing from self-centered life to God-centered life

 2. Changing from a chaotic life to a contented life

 3. Changing from an earthly centered success to a heavenly centered success

II. Freedom from Sticky Situations of Life by Listening to Jesus

A. Listening involves where to invest one's life.

B. Listening involves where to invest one's priority.

 1. Priority of God

 2. Priority of family

 3. Priority of church

 4. Priority of job

     5. Priority of others

     6. Priority of self

  C. Listening involves encouragement and hope.

  D. Listening involves determination.

  E. Listening involves blessed assurance.

III. Freedom from Sticky Situations of Life Introduces Joy in Jesus

  A. Joy for the divine resource of life

  B. Joy for the "hallelujahs" of life

     It was difficult for the teacher, but the circumstances were a bit unusual. A kid in the class kept disrupting the whole classroom of other children with his "hallelujahs." He did it once too often, and off he went to the principal's office. The busy principal gave the boy a geography book to look at, thinking that there was nothing worth a hallelujah on the pages. Suddenly without warning the principal heard a loud "hallelujah" and dashed over to see what made the boy get all excited.

     He asked the child what created this need for shouting "hallelujah." The boy replied, "I was just reading in this geography book about oceans, and I came to a sentence which says that the depth of some seas has not been discovered, and my Bible says that my sins have been cast into the depth of the sea—hallelujah!"[2]

  C. Joy for living for the world to come

  D. Joy for the holy presence of God

Conclusion

    Freedom is getting loose from the sticky situations of life. Are you free?

---

1. Source unknown. Found in author's files without source.

2. Leslie Flynn, *Come Alive with Illustrations* (Grand Rapids: Baker Book House, 1988), 157.

I Love a Parade

Luke 19:28-44

Introduction

The atmosphere was at a carnival pitch. Noise emanated from everywhere as people talked with strong feelings, exuberance, and emotion. Can you picture yourself there that Palm Sunday day? Can you feel the pulse of the emotions? Suddenly there is a jerky motion as the parade begins. Spontaneously people began to put their coats down while others tore off branches from the palm trees to lay in front of the donkey carrying Jesus of Nazareth. The people needed to vent their feelings of frustration with the government of Rome and their own ruling 70 and their reign of tyranny. They saw in Jesus the end of that political intrigue and the end of Roman rule and the end of their own bondage. They mistook the donkey that symbolized peace for the white steed of war. Their unorganized chaos becomes a controlled chorus of "hallelujahs" to their hope—Jesus.

Oh, what a beautiful morning—oh, what a beautiful day! The sun shone brightly and the emotions of the crowd matched the sun. In the middle of the excitement no one noticed the tears in the eyes of Jesus or heard the soft weeping sounds.

There are some lessons in this scripture passage.

I. The Parade Preparations

When I was in high school I marched in the American Royal Parade with my high school band. It was an exciting time. My band teacher, A. T. Estes, spent weeks drilling us in marching and preparing us to play the music. When the day arrived, we were bussed from Turner High School to our assigned location. The band members looked sharp in our black and gold band uniforms and white spats atop our black shoes. Even as a young person I was amazed at all the preparation that went into the organization of the parade. All the bands had a particular spot, the horse units each were placed in various locations in the route (usually just ahead of the bands). Everyone and everything had its place.

It didn't magically come together. There was a master plan by the organizers of the parade.

Most commentators agree that Jesus orchestrated His entrance into Jerusalem. Biblical commentator Bruce Larsen spelled it out, "Are you aware that Jesus planned His own parade? He didn't wait for his loyal friends to give Him a gold watch . . . He needed this parade unashamedly for his own sake, as well as for the sake of His followers, then and now."[1]

Jesus sent two of His disciples for the float and they came back with a donkey. Even that was planned! Christ had given them a password, "The Lord has need," if they were questioned as to why the donkey was being taken.

In today's chaotic, frightening world Jesus is sending His disciples to make ready His triumphal entrance into the Holy City. Jesus is coming again and will be the Grand Marshal at His own parade!

II. Jesus Is Preparing for This Parade and It Will Occur

A. He has declared the parade will begin (John 14:1-3).
B. His disciples have declared that the parade will begin.
C. His history has declared that the parade will begin.

There is a constant movement toward a climax of history. Is it any wonder that Jesus looked over Jerusalem and wept? Jerusalem represents our world today. He may be weeping over us now, but there is coming a day when the weeping will be done and the shouting will begin!

III. The Parade Route

A. Along the parade route were the disenfranchised of society.
B. Along the parade route were the families of Israel.
C. Along the parade route were the people healed by His love.
D. Along the parade route were the disciples.
E. Along the parade route were the Pharisees of life.

I once received a letter from Charles Swindoll when he was a pastor. The stationery impressed me, for it had the faces of people as the header. I don't know if it was people from his congregation or not, but it made an impression on me. That is what the church is all about—people finding Jesus along the parade route.

IV. The Parade's Grand Marshal

A. Jesus is the center of excitement.

B. Jesus is the center of response.

C. Jesus is the center of controversy.

D. Jesus is the center of the needy.

E. Jesus is the center of life.

Jesus can take no other place in the parade of life. You cannot shove Him out of the way—He will not take a back row spot. Jesus must be the Grand Marshal. He is the reason for the parade!

Conclusion

At the end of his comments, Larsen writes, "The original Palm Sunday parade was primarily for Jesus, but it was also for the disciples. It was for the crowd, offering them one more chance to respond to the King. The parade was for you and me because Jesus is still passing by in your life and mine, giving us one more chance to say, 'Yes, I want what You offer.' Or, 'No, deal me out.'"[2]

Come on, friend, get in the parade with Jesus!

---

1. Bruce Larsen, *Communicator's Commentary* (Waco: Word Publisher, 1983), 281.

2. Ibid., 284.

Spiritual Survival Tactics

Luke 21:5-28

Introduction

The Pacific theater of war was desperately bleak during the spring of 1942. One island after another fell like lined-up dominoes. The Japanese army was marching into the Philippines, confident and methodically ready to snatch victory from the allied hands. On March 11, 1942, General Douglas MacArthur was forced to escape to Australia lest he be captured. As he stepped into the boat destined for safety on March 11, 1942, he uttered those now famous three words, "I SHALL RETURN."

The countries of the world slugged it out on the world fronts—Allied Forces versus the Axis Forces. It took a bit over two and a half years, but on October 20, 1944, MacArthur stepped out from a boat onto Philippine soil and uttered another three-word phrase, "I HAVE RETURNED."

General MacArthur kept his word to the Filipino people even against the most difficult odds imaginable. The general had some important survival tactics in operation in order to return and they succeeded.

Part of the good news of the gospel is that Jesus will keep His word to the people of the world. Think of all the odds against Jesus and the possibilities of His spiritual survival.

1. His birth to poverty-ridden Jewish subjects
2. His birthplace and hometown in a small obscure village
3. His time in history where there was no instant communication technology
4. His selection of followers who were fickle and fearful
5. His opposition by spiritual and political leadership
6. His punishment and death on a cross

All of these obstacles to His declaration to returning to earth, but though He died He did return to earth. He was the victor over death, sin, Satan, and hell! He left to return to heaven, but once again He will come back to earth. This time it will be in power and glory. Each citizen of earth who has a personal relationship with Him should stand and shout, "GLORY TO GOD!"

Until the time of His ultimate arrival we are still earthbound but not left powerless. We must have a spiritual survival tactic that will propel us into the days ahead.

I. Spiritual Survival Depends upon Following Truly Spiritual Leaders

A. Leaders whose lives are holy
B. Leaders whose lives are honest
C. Leaders whose lives are truly devout
D. Leaders whose lives are earnest in motive
E. Leaders whose lives are disciplined in their work ethic
F. Leaders whose lives are courageous in their faith
G. Leaders whose lives model spirituality to others

Dr. John Bowling, president of Olivet Nazarene University in Bourbonnais, Illinois, writes, "Grace-full leadership brings into view something different than the styles so prevalent in leadership literature. Focusing on spirit rather than style strengthens the concept that the leader is not preoccupied with conformity for conformity's sake but rather creating a vision-centered environment where objectives and expectations are met through the efforts of individuals who don't just work for the company but are the company.

"The real power and energy of grace-full leaders rests in the relationship of both the leader and the followers to a commonly held set of values and objectives instead of merely the relation of the leader to the follower.

"A focus on spirit more than style implies that leadership must be value-centered."[1]

II. Spiritual Survival Depends on the Excitement of the Jesus Revolution of the Future

A. The revolution is written about in the apocalyptic literature of the Bible.
B. The revolution is for the person who is redeemed by the blood of Jesus.
C. The revolution will transform the world as we now know it.
D. The revolution will be for those who watch and pray.
E. The revolution will come! It is inevitable.

F. The revolution is a time of spiritual excitement when Jesus frees us from the bondage of this world.

III. Spiritual Survival Depends on the Hope of the Future

    A. Spiritual hope is seen in the testimony of the believer.
1. That testimony includes our journey of faith.
2. That testimony includes the logic of your faith.
3. That testimony includes the clear reality of your faith.
4. That testimony includes the practicality of your faith.
5. That testimony includes the mysticism of your faith.
6. That testimony includes the genuineness of your faith.

    B. Spiritual hope is seen in the optimism of the future.

    C. Spiritual hope is seen in the purpose of the future.

    D. Spiritual hope is seen in the eternity of the future.

Conclusion

Ellyn Sanna wrote: "Sometimes I feel as though my life has been swallowed up by dark storms. Troubles and overwhelming responsibilities press so close around me that they seem to block the sun, and I stumble in the dark, not certain if I am going anywhere at all or only traveling in circles. But if I lift my head and look, I find that Christ's light burns before me, high and lifted up, its radiance as bright as ever. No regrets over the past, no worries for today, no fears about the future can ever dim that light. All I have to do is look at Him—and He will guide me out of the storms, into the safe harbor of His love."[2]

My future is in the hope I now have in Christ. Let that be your hope!

---

1. John Bowling, *Grace-Full Leadership* (Kansas City: Beacon Hill Press of Kansas City, 2000), 16.
2. Sanna, *A Beacon of Hope,* 14.

Role Models

Luke 22:7-20

Introduction

A new theatrical play was introduced to audiences in London written by Sir James Barrie. Parents were upset with his new play and demanded changes be made because it was literally endangering the children of England. The play was *Peter Pan* and in the original version, Peter Pan told the Darling children that if they believed strong enough that they would be able to take to the air and fly! The young English children took Peter Pan's words literally and they began attempting to fly from sofas, windows, tables, and trees. They were injuring themselves by the hundreds. When the parents' requests came, Sir Barrie unhesitatingly altered the script to include a cautionary statement that children could fly, but only if they had been first sprinkled with "fairy dust."[1]

Peter Pan was a role model for the English children in 1904. Who or what today has become role models for our children? As I write this Bill Gates has been interviewed with his new video games that are rated XXX for adults. The problem is they have been circulated among the children. A report for Christmas 2002 indicates that the fastest selling video games among children feature the pornographic, sex, violence agendas.

Graphic statistics reveal the alarming rapidity of America turning away from the Christian faith. According to Thom Rainer, dean of the Billy Graham School of Missions, Evangelism and Church Growth, Southern Baptist Theological Seminary, Louisville, Kentucky, said that in a random telephone survey of 1,300 people that researchers talked to four generations of Americans. He identified them categorically as builders (born before 1946), boomers (born between 1946 and 1964), busters (born between 1965 and 1976), and bridgers (born between 1977 and 1994). He said that out of the 1,300 surveyed he was "alarmed by the low percentage of people in each group who responded that they considered themselves Christians based on having accepted Christ as personal Savior." He disclosed that of the builder generation, 65 percent were Christians; boomer generation, 35 percent; buster generation, 15 percent; and bridger generation only 4 percent. Another astounding statistic reveals of these folks, 75 percent became Christians before the age of 14.[2]

The church, Christians, and parents have allowed Hollywood, sports figures, musicians, wrestlers, and others to influence us rather than the heroes of the faith. My concern is that we remember that it is not too late to influence through Christian modeling, responsible behavior, moral standards, Christian morality, and transparent, authentic, Christ-centered faith before children and nonbelieving adults!

I. Role Modeling Begins in Christians of the Faith

  A. Bible characters leap off the pages of the Bible to give guidance.
   1. Moses
   2. Joshua
   3. Peter
  B. Christians leap off the pages of history to give guidance.
   1. Martin Luther
   2. John Wesley
   3. William Booth
  C. Christians of today to give guidance
   1. Billy Graham
   2. Chuck Swindoll
   3. Lloyd Ogilvie

II. Role Modeling Shares Common Characteristics

  A. They have a firm faith that doesn't give way.
  B. They have a firm compassion for all people.
  C. They have a faith that responds automatically to needs.
  D. They have a faith that involves themselves in the burdens of others.
  E. They have a faith that reaches down to help people to climb out of the evils of life to the goodness of life.
  F. They have a faith that is sold out 100 percent to God.
      Several years ago my wife and I attended our denominational meetings in San Antonio, Texas. While there we visited the Alamo. It was there that 183 men defended the Alamo against the onslaught of thousands of Mexican troops. Two hours before the sun set on March 3,

1836, the Mexican artillery went silent. During the lull in the battle it became apparent that the garrison was doomed. William Travis called his men together in a single line formation inside the walls surrounding the old Catholic church building. He explained to them that no reinforcements were coming to their aid and that their destiny was sealed. Like the biblical Joshua, he pulled his sword and drew a line in the dirt and asked every man who was determined to fight for the independence of Texas and to die to cross the line. According to tradition the first man to cross the line was Topley Holland and he was quickly followed by Daniel Cloud, Micajah Utry, Davy Crockett, and the rest of the doomed troopers. Wounded Commander of the Alamo, Jim Bowie, called for help to cross the line and four men jumped to his side and carried his cot over the line to the cheers of the ragged men. On March 6, just three days later, all of the men died. They made the choice 72 hours earlier that counted most and the Republic of Texas was birthed from their shed blood.

How many of us are ready to commit mind, body, soul, and spirit to be role models for this generation and the ones to follow?

III. Role Modeling Seeks People to Become Role Models

A. Others to take up the mantel of caring
B. Others to go the distance
C. Others to commit to a spiritually hero-starved world
D. Others to see the need
E. Others to hold up the truth despite rejection

Conclusion

Will you be one that Jesus can count on to be a role model to a world so desperately in need of Him?

---

1. King Duncan, *Dynamic Preaching Magazine,* April 1995, Vol. 10, No. 4 (Knoxville, Tenn.: Seven Worlds Pub.), 190.

2. From an article on the LifeWay Internet page titled "Churches Reaching Children Implement Intentional Strategies" in an archive news release—October 2000. Go to: www.lifeway.com/about_1000g.asp

Jesus Reaches a Searching Heart

Luke 23:39-43

Introduction

The crucifixion of Jesus is an emotionally charged scene. Leading up this point has been a mock trial before the Jewish Sanhedrin. Jesus has appeared before the Roman political leader Pontius Pilate, who could find no fault in Christ. Even Pilate's wife has made an appearance begging for Jesus' release and telling her husband to have nothing to do with His penalty. Pilate dramatically has a basin of water brought out to where he washes his hands and declares loudly that what the people do with Jesus he personally disavows any responsibility for, but hands Christ over to die. Before the Lord is taken to Golgotha He is flogged, mocked by the soldiers, and has a crown of thorns roughly placed on His head. He has been paraded down the streets of Jerusalem amid the jeers and chants of an ungodly people. After arriving at the Place of the Skull a soldier pushes Him down on a splintery cross and another takes a long spike and begins hammering it into His flesh as the blood splatters on his military tunic and Jesus cries out in pain. Several soldiers then come and pick up the Cross with its divine/human cargo and plunge it unmercifully hard into the hole dug specifically for it. Emotions ran so high as His loving mother stood by and watched the proceeding, as did several other women and John. The moments ticked by like eternity. Bored with it all, someone begins the mocking of His claim of Messiahship. It's at this point we stop and examine the scene. Two men, thieves according to the Scripture, are placed on either side of Him. One jeers with the crowd, while the other ponders eternity. Today are you jeering Jesus or pondering the eternity of life?

I. The Unrepentant Thief (v. 39)

A. He was unresponsive to Christ.

Someone remarked that sin is not what keeps us from God; it is really our inability to respond to the love that God offers. What things keep you from responding to God's love?

1. Is it some unexplainable crisis that we blame God for that keeps us from Him?
2. Is it unexplainable circumstances that we blame God for that keep us from Him?
3. Is it that we have lost our trust in people that has transferred to a lack of trust in God that keeps us from Him?
4. Is it that we have lost our true image of the living God and picture Him as a false Father image that keeps us from Him?

B. He had hardened his heart habitually.
C. He had refused to believe Jesus is spite of the signs.
   1. There was no repentance in his attitude.
   2. There was no love in his attitude.
   3. There was no listening even to the testimony of the other thief in his attitude.
   4. There was no faith even when he heard Jesus say to the other thief, "Paradise is yours today." What is keeping *you* from Jesus?
D. He had no guarantee of eternal life.

II. The Repentant Thief (v. 42)

A. He recognized he was a sinner (v. 41).
   1. He was in the "habit" of sinning.
   2. He was separated from God.
   3. He was lost in this world.
B. He recognized his need to respond to Jesus.
   1. He recognized who Jesus was on the Cross.
   2. He confessed his sin to Jesus even on the cross.
      a. He is the prime example that salvation is not by works.
      b. He is the prime example that salvation is by faith.
C. He accepted the opportunity to repent.
D. He received Christ's guarantee of paradise.

III. Jesus the Savior

A. Willing to reach out even in His agony
B. Willing to love even in His agony
C. Willing to save even in His agony
D. Willing to die even in His agony

Conclusion

The story is told that when slaves were being brought to America by the Portuguese that a slave ship came under attack by an English vessel. The chase lasted for hours when finally the English ship came next to the Portuguese sailing ship. The captain of the slave ship gave guns to the slaves and told them that the English were their enemies and to fight. The terrified slaves began shooting the very people who had come to rescue them. Jesus came to set the captives of sin free, but the Pharisees rose against Jesus; and the very men He loved and came to free killed Him. Jesus came to save you and me. He was willing to die for you and me. Don't be like the one thief on the cross and reject Christ's offer!

Rolling Stones

Luke 24:1-11

Introduction

The ladies who were close to Jesus wanted to do one last act of love for Him. They had watched aghast at the horrible scene on Friday as Jesus was crucified. Joseph of Arimathea had taken the body of Jesus and laid it in his own tomb where his family was to be buried. Since the Sabbath day was quickly approaching, it was a hurry-up burial with little preparation of the body. It was because of the quickness of it all that we now have this scene with the women coming to the tomb. As they walk toward the burial scene one of them remembered the stone—this huge stone that literally weighed a ton—who would roll the stone back from the entrance? Reality set in. As the tomb came into view, they were surprised that the stone had already been moved!

Today many have stones blocking our entrance to the miracle of the resurrection.

I. Stone One Is Lack of Direction (vv. 1-2)

God has given us a map for this life's direction that will get us to the end of our journey in the next.

A. His map includes guidance in this life. Richard Taylor wrote some rules for guidance.
   1. Don't try to reproduce anyone else's guidance in your life.
   2. Don't expect everyday occurrences of dramatic guidance.
   3. Don't ask for special guidance about plain duties. Instead, pray for grace to do them faithfully.
   4. Learn experientially the full meaning of peace in the heart.
   5. Do not act hastily.
   6. Do not be too cast down when you have reason to believe that you have missed the Holy Spirit's signal. He will let you know and you can change and learn by the experience.
   7. Keep on praying for guidance.[1]

B. His map includes acquaintance with God.

C. His map includes purpose in life for God.

D. His map includes a heart explored for God
   1. A heart exploring salvation
   2. A heart exploring sanctification
   3. A heart exploring maturity

II. Stone Two Is Confusion (vv. 3-4)

Many people of this world are confused.

A. They are confused about real love.

B. They are confused about real charity.

C. They are confused about godly ambition.

D. They are confused about real truth.

E. They are confused about real holiness.

F. They are confused about living.

These women were confused, but their confusion became clear understanding later. God wants to do that in our lives—give us clear understanding.

III. Stone Three Is How to Worship (vv. 5-8)

The women stood in holy terror at the dazzling light coming from the angels. Too often we stand unaffected by the dazzling light of a Holy God with His Shechinah glory. We take Him for granted. Worship has become routine, boring, and unenthusiastic. No longer do we boldly sing, "Love so amazing, so divine, demands my life, my soul, my all." No longer are we lost in wonder, love, and praise. No longer is there inexpressible joy upon our faces or wonder in our eyes!

Worship should include the following:

A. Acknowledging Him

B. Listening to Him

C. Standing amazed at Him

D. Praying to Him

E. Reading the love letter from Him

F. Patiently waiting for Him

G. Welcoming Him

H. Living for Him

I. Surrendering to Him

J. Obeying Him

IV. Stone Four Is Unbelief

Mary Magdalene, Joanna, Mary, the mother of James and John, and the other women told the amazing story of the stone being rolled away. The disciples scoffed but sent Peter and John to verify the story. The two arrived and discovered the women's story to be true!

A. Unbelief can be turned into faith by focusing on God.

B. Unbelief can be turned into faith by answering the call of God.

C. Unbelief can be turned into faith by interpreting the message of God.

D. Unbelief can be turned into faith by thankfully receiving the life of God.

E. Unbelief can be turned into faith by handing life over to God.

Conclusion

I heard about a pastor who had taken some pictures while on a fishing expedition in the Gulf of Mexico. He was awed by the sunrises and the sunsets over the gulf and caught them on film. When he arrived home and had the film developed he made a discovery. He could no longer tell which were the sunrises and which were the sunsets.

Thanks to the empty tomb, death is like that for the one who is a believer. To many it appears to be an end: the end of a life, the end of a relationship, a time of desperation and sadness—a sunset. But for those who believe in Jesus it is a new beginning—a sunrise.

---

1. Richard S. Taylor, *Life in the Spirit* (Kansas City: Beacon Hill Press of Kansas City, 1966), 146-48.

Communion Thoughts

Luke 24:13-35

Introduction
"Near Stroudsburg, Pennsylvania, lies the grave of an unknown but greatly celebrated soldier. His gravestone bears these words: 'Abraham Lincoln's substitute.' Amid the anguish and tragedy of America's Civil War, President Lincoln chose to honor this man by naming him as his representative. In so doing, the president made that man a symbol of the fact that each soldier who perished on the battlefields was dying that others might live."[1]

The essence of the Lord's Supper is the reminder that Jesus died that we might live. All Christian traditions grasp the importance of the fact of Christ's death for the world.

I. The Disciples Were in a Swirl of Activity (vv. 14-15)
A. These disciples were coming from a swirl of horrendous activities.
  1. There had been the arrest of Jesus.
  2. There had been the mock trial of Jesus.
  3. There had been the crucifixion of Jesus.
B. These disciples were coming to grips with "business as usual" or "back to the routine."
C. These disciples were on their way "somewhere."
D. These disciples were interrupted in their business.
E. These disciples were in the midst of theological discussion and almost missed the presence of Jesus.

   We are a lot like those disciples. We get so busy with the state of affairs that we are involved in that we forget the why of our business. We "steal" minutes of the day in order to be with Him or His Word. The truth is that for many even when we are "stealing" the moments our thoughts are elsewhere. Communion is a visual aid that reminds us that in our swirl of activity God still wants to meet us. He still has time for us. He still loves us.

II. The Disciples Were in an Emotionally Depressive State (vv. 17-21)

A. These disciples were on an emotional roller coaster.
1. They were high on Palm Sunday.
2. They were down on Good Friday.
3. They were midride on sullen Saturday.
B. These disciples were like modern-day disciples who go on the roller coaster ride too.
C. These disciples were to learn they could not lean on emotions—nor can modern-day disciples.
D. Communion draws us back to the reality of fact and faith
1. Fact is—Jesus died.
2. Fact is—Jesus went to hell to preach.
3. Fact is—Jesus arose from the grave.
4. Fact is—Jesus is alive.
5. Fact is—I believe it.

III. The Disciples Were in a Confused State (vv. 22-24)

A. They were in a confused state because of their swirl of activity.
B. They were in a confused state because of their emotional depression.
C. They were in a confused state because of their spiritual immaturity.
D. They were in a confused state because of their preconceived ideas.

IV. The Disciples Were to Come to the Light (vv. 25-32)

A. Jesus instructed them in the light.
B. Jesus helped them see the light.
C. Jesus overcame their darkness of heart by giving them the light.
D. Jesus showed them humility and suffering was a part of the light.
E. Jesus is the light.

V. The Disciples Were Compelled to Share Their Experience (vv. 33-35)

A. Their experience included a message of hope.
B. Their experience included a message of joy.

C. Their experience included a message of fellowship.

D. Their experience included a message of spreading the good news through evangelism.

It was a long seven miles in a depressed state to Emmaus. It was a quick, lighthearted seven miles back to Jerusalem, because they simply could not keep the good news to themselves. The Christian message is never fully ours until we have shared it with someone else.

Conclusion

Communion is a demonstration of fellowship and sharing in the passing of the bread and juice—symbols of sharing His body and blood, His work and life.

Leonard Fein in a baccalaureate address at Stanford University asked, "Do you remember Raoul Wallenberg? He is one of the heroes of the 20th century we dare not forget." During the waning days of 1944, the Third Reich knew they were losing the war and were frantically rushing more than 100,000 Jews from Budapest to their deaths in the concentration camps. Another 100,000 from Budapest were spared and survived the war, mostly through the audacity and bravery of this single Swedish diplomat, Raoul Wallenberg.

Wallenberg worked feverishly. Rushing to the train station at the time of deportation, he would separate those Jews carrying Swedish passports. The Nazi military never knew that these Swedish passports were forgeries that Wallenberg had made. More than once, Raoul intercepted a transport train, or followed the route of the Nazis' murderous midwinter, 200-mile death march to take people out of harm's way.

Someone asked, "Can you imagine that? One man saving thousands of others—not even of his faith? How did he do it? I believe God was with him. It is one thing to say, 'God is on our side' when you are waging war. It is quite another to say, 'God is on our side' when you are risking your own life to save others."[2]

Communion is a reminder that this is precisely what Jesus did for each of us. He not only risked His life, but He died for us.

---

1. Richard Bodey and Robert Holmes, eds., *Come to the Banquet* (Grand Rapids: Baker Books, 1998), 9.

2. C. King Duncan, ed., *Dynamic Preaching Magazine,* Vol. 18, No. 1, Jan.-Mar., 2003, 82.